back in america

Books by Barry Gifford

FICTION
Do the Blind Dream?
American Falls:
The Collected Short Stories
Wyoming
My Last Martini
The Sinaloa Story
Baby Cat-Face
Arise and Walk
Night People
Port Tropique
Landscape with Traveler
A Boy's Novel
The Sailor and Lula Novels:
Wild at Heart
Perdita Durango
Sailor's Holiday
Sultans of Africa
Consuelo's Kiss
Bad Day for the Leopard Man

NON-FICTION
Brando Rides Alone
Out of the Past:
Adventures in Film Noir
Las cuatro reinas (with David Perry)
Bordertown (with David Perry)
The Phantom Father: A Memoir
A Day at the Races:
The Education of a Racetracker
Saroyan: A Biography
(with Lawrence Lee)
The Neighborhood of Baseball
Jack's Book: An Oral Biography of Jack Kerouac (with Lawrence Lee)
Read 'Em and Weep:
My Favorite Novels

POETRY
Back in America
Replies to Wang Wei
Ghosts No Horse Can Carry
Giotto's Circle
Flaubert at Key West
Beautiful Phantoms
Horse hauling timber out of Hokkaido forest
Poems from Snail Hut
Persimmons: Poems for Paintings
Selected Poems of Francis Jammes (translations with Bettina Dickie)
The Boy You Have Always Loved
Coyote Tantras
The Blood of the Parade

PLAYS
Hotel Room Trilogy

SCREENPLAY
Lost Highway
(with David Lynch)

ANTHOLOGY
The Rooster Trapped in the Reptile Room: A BARRY GIFFORD READER

back in america

new poems

Barry Gifford

Manufactured in the United States of America

Cover and Book Design by Joshua Clark
Cover photograph by David Perry

Light of New Orleans Publishing, LLC
828 Royal Street, Suite 307
New Orleans, Louisiana 70116

www.frenchquarterfiction.com

ACKNOWLEDGMENTS

Some of these poems have previously appeared in the following publications: *Shenandoah, First Intensity, Quiksilver, Booglit, Poetry Flash, Exquisite Corpse, Tarpaulin Sky, Fandango* (Rome), *Cuadrilátero* (Madrid), *Panta* (Milan), *Madame Class* (Milan), *Bordertown* (Chronicle Books, San Francisco), *Romania Literara* (Bucharest), and *Handshake Editions* (Paris). "The Last Words of Arthur Rimbaud" was published in a limited edition by The Bancroft Library Press (University of California, 1998).

Library of Congress Cataloging-in-Publication Data

Gifford, Barry, 1946-
Back in America : new poems / Barry Gifford.
p. cm.
LCCN 2004006933
ISBN 0-9714076-4-9 (pbk. : alk. paper)
I. Title.
PS3557.I283B335 2004
811'.54--dc22

contents

This book is dedicated to the poets
Agustín Lara, Smokey Robinson,
Don Covay, Hoagy Carmichael, and
Boudleaux and Felice Bryant.

For Brother Ray, still traveling

1

Back in America

back in america

Old cowboy
crossing Oakland
street
with rodeo limp,
spotted face
and hands
boots scuffed, cracked
filthy shirt
untucked—
stuffed in left
back pocket
of faded jeans
The Iliad—
if only Homer
could see him,
headed
to dump hotel
half-pint
of bad bourbon
in bag
dreaming glories
of Greece
and his
lost
horse

on viewing the manuscript scroll of jack kerouac's novel *On the Road* in the tosca bar, san francisco

---

Lying in state, under glass,
partially unrolled to reveal
flood of words describ'd
Mississippi River near New Orleans
1947—an American Shroud,
Davia Nelson called it, like
the Shroud of Turin, holy remnant
of modern Literature, naively
woven tapestry—
Kerouac would have lov'd
this I think, his own worn
Shrouded Stranger, well-travel'd
displayed for religious purpose,
himself collapsed Catholic Buddhist
pilgrim in constant search
for the Sacred, sanctified today
here in sere mute Tosca cathedral
light, lone silver'd stream of sun,
God's finger pointed toward window
sarcophagus casket containing
phantom tome brought out by hand
half-century before by Jack Kerouac
from America's burning Egyptian heart.

10 may 2001

small elegy for Corso *to Fernanda Pivano*

Gregory Corso's buried in Rome
a few weeks ago next to Shelley
in an *acattòlico* cemetery in Testaccio
Sitting on a bench in the Piazza Cavour
I recall Nanda telling me last December
Gregory had his balls cut off
"I don't care," he told her, "I fucked enough."
Now at twilight in the Quartiere Prati
watching rich women walk big dogs
past palm trees under plum-colored sky
suddenly there's Corso ten years ago or more
at a baseball game in San Francisco
shouting at a player, "Pull up your pants!
It's a disgrace to the uniform!"
Three rows in front I looked around,
"Gregory," I said, "what happened to
your teeth?" "They're gone!" he said
"Who needs teeth after fifty?"
We met again at a wedding in Bolinas
Quietly he told me how secretly he
envied Kerouac having died so young,
only 47. "If only he could have enjoyed
himself more, but he was always drunk."

(cont.)

O Gregory, may you take eternity for all
it's worth, the same as you captured
your time on earth, knowing all along
there was nothing real to lose.
Roll over, Captain Poetry,
tell old Percy the news.

25 May 2001

in memory of Suwa Yu

Creek
crawling through
woods
How many thousands
of years
without stopping
I'm happy
to listen
longer
than that

the day Allen Ginsberg died

I got up early
looked out the window
at a freight passing
on the Hudson
sun poking out
reluctantly, a colder day
than expected
I'd heard the night before
Allen was sick and dying
given only a few
months to live
Odd to find myself
in New York, his city
at the moment
of his passing
The newspaper said
he had recently completed
a new book entitled
Death and Fame
This afternoon I visited
one of my oldest
and best friends
who a few days before
had told me his father
was not expected to live
more than a few weeks

His father was
a tough guy
I'd always liked him
a working class guy
from Chicago
where he still lived
His son called him
while I was there
and handed me the phone
The old man sounded
as strong as he always
had—difficult for me
to believe he'd soon
be gone
He called me by a
childhood name
and suddenly
I teared up
No way to stop this
I thought.
Now Allen G. dead
gone to greet
Jack and Neal
after almost thirty years
I imagine Jack
in Buddha Heaven
saying, Thanks for
coming, Al
This morning is his funeral

(cont.)

I decide not to go
figuring it will be
a mob scene
I don't like funerals
anyway and what's
the point
At nine a.m.
when the Buddhist ceremony
is scheduled to begin
a four hour affair
culminating in cremation
the doorbell rings
I have a vision of Allen
standing at the door
saying, I didn't die
but I don't want to miss
this. Come with me!
But instead it's
the plumber
I first met Allen
thirty-one years ago
in London
He'd come with his
father Louis to give
a poetry reading
A few years later
we worked together
editing a book
of his and Neal's letters
I last saw him
two years ago

in Paris
We met on the
rue de Sèvres
he showed me a medal
the French minister
of culture
had awarded him
He told me
how good I looked
kissed me wetly
on both cheeks
Allen wrote
Death stay thy phantoms!
and was alloted his
three score and ten
He and Kerouac
were two of
my greatest inspirations
when I was a kid
They gave me hope
that beauty and meaning
could be found
amid the chaos
I told him
this once
and Allen said
Keep hoping!
Hiking together
on a trail

(cont.)

at Gary Snyder's
Kitkitdizze in 1976
we came upon
a pile of ashes
and stepped carefully
around them
Allen's ashes
are to be buried
by Louis's grave
In death we return
to the father
Farewell Allen
you're with
the phantoms now.

reminder to myself

Just realized
April 5 is a bad day
Larry Lee died age 48
that date 1990
Allen Ginsberg died age 70
that date 1997
I was in New York both times
on my way to France
when Larry passed
in hospital San Francisco
AIDS diagnosed six months before
"I could die from a cat scratch"
he said our last lunch
together
Allen died in New York
I was at Marshall's
when Gus Van Sant called
to tell me
"It'll be a Buddhist funeral"
he said "Will you go?"
I didn't, wrote a poem
for Allen instead
I'd known him more than 30 years
I remember Allen's comment
about Larry (1976)
"too *Time* magazine"

(cont.)

questioning his sympathies
when we were writing *Jack's Book*
thinking Larry
not sufficiently on
"our" side
Told Allen he was wrong,
Larry was *rara avis*
an objective journalist
told him not to worry
"protecting" Kerouac
with revisionist tactics won't work
in the long run anyway
better let people say
what they want, not manipulate
Later, after he'd read the manuscript
Allen said "It's just like
Rashomon —
everybody lies
and the truth
comes out!"
Larry loved Kerouac and Allen, too
He died alone, drowned by
his own fluids
only nurse stranger near
Allen fell into coma, corroded
by cancer, attended by friends
In his final poem
mentioned Kerouac, wrote
"No more Sunset Boulevard"
Larry choked out last words:
"Is this it?"

Mr. Demille, stay thy camera—
I'm not ready
for my close-up
just yet

airplane Milan-San Francisco
31 August 1999

bordertown

Bordertown

is a place to make money,
spectacles to
attract tourists,
a sopa picante with
a touch
of evil

****

Man knifed on Juarez
sidestreet,
stiff after
two days,
his stink
not even noticeable
or defined among the
general stench
by Club Colorada
A miniature Yolanda all
mouth and eyes
shimmering in
a doorway

****

Bordertown is the city of spooks,
of greedy ghosts
and unapproachable
visions

****

Dirt streets of
deep southwest,
pariah dogs groan
in the fabulous dust
and heat,
flies laying eggs
on chickens
and hanging
pigs

******

The only certainty is
at the cemeteries, the
only grip
on life to visit and
revisit
the acknowledged dead
The living dead pay homage
to each other's fate,

(cont.)

a place to
finally meet
and be restful

Impossible to be at
peace
in this crush,
this pesthole
life built
on the refuse of
El Norte

*****

Whores in the broken
light like
giant parrots,
birds ready
to peck your eyes
and pick your pockets
At the same time
become dreamy
Aztec princesses muy sincero
y las románticas
de sus sueños

*****

The ramshackle countryside
devours the border sun,

thin wind
tickles scabrous brush
as border patrol run down
rats scurrying
from the rotten
stinking sinking
ship
like piñatas falling
off the back
of a speeding
truck

*****

Here's where the road
ends,
in the ground or at water's edge—
Boca Chica, the girl's
mouth,
the gates
of hell
or heaven
swung
wide,
waiting to
receive you,

the same in death
as in life,
forever.

rainy tijuana

Riding slow in taxi
rainy night Tijuana
tiny whore
red skirt
tilting
on spike heels
darts pink tongue
through
silver paint lips
her bare
bird shoulders
make me shiver

monk in the morning

for Al Young

I love to listen to Monk
in the morning
Those tilted notes
hit me
just right
It's the way I feel
before the world
gets into
my head
pulls me
kicking and screaming
out of those
brilliant corners
"Coming on the Hudson"
is my speed
slow blue steps
up toward
as much consciousness
as I can handle
Monk's music is stolen
from dreams
anyway
Only Thelonious
could get through that
door
the only one
with the right
key

american music

Dusk, Oakland—
girl in window
leaning on a pillow, smoking
she resembles
Billie Holiday
four flights up
pudgy, bored
exhaling desire
into the already fetid
late summer air

shanghai garden

I'd be confined
to dreams
were it
not
for the
blue dragonfly
just landed
on
my hand

chinatown carnival night

Wizened Chinese bum
slumped on bench
grimy sack by sandaled feet
toes torn and black
Portsmouth Square San Francisco
bloodflecked beard
oozing eyes
surrounded by people
passing unseeing
lost from their world
suffering this last indignity
going soon to drink
endless cups of rice wine
in the better company
of heavenly dragons

change in the weather

For years I was lost
in the eye of a hurricane
rain and wind enshrouded my heart
I couldn't see beyond the clouds
Now the sky's brightness
almost blinds me
but sometimes I catch you
hiding behind your eyes
the most beautiful eyes
I've ever seen
I kiss them tenderly
hoping you'll allow me
to see you as nobody else
not even you
ever has

september 11, 2001

The Chinese
used
to say
in parting
from a person
perceived
as an
adversary
"May you live
in interesting
times."
This is
our new
address

late september in toronto
and the weather is still fair

———

I love these
young girls
proud
of
their breasts
As we pass
on the street
they confess
everything,
knowing how
easy it is
for me
to forgive
them

adios, chico!

Kid Gavilian is dead
in Miami, a Cubano welter
who couldn't beat Sugar Ray,
not in New York, anyway—
He had a bolo
but no real punch, and
a face like a frying pan
full of sizzling
chicken livers

Eurydice in Romania

Gorgeous Gypsy girl, perhaps
fifteen or sixteen,
wrapped in a silver and black
striped strapless dress,
wearing high heels, big sunglasses,
waist-length cobalt hair
brushed by the breeze, strolling
next to the narrow, crumbling highway—
Is she a prostitute? I think not,
just a kid done up on
a boring Sunday afternoon—
she could be on a runway in Milan,
strutting for Valentino,
instead of parading in the drizzle
on a lonely road
through the Carpathian mountains—
I look back, but
she's disappeared
and I hate that I'll never
see her again.

near Vatra Dornei,
1 June 03

2

Shooting Pool in the Dark

rue des abbesses

Beauty will drive
you mad
it'll tear
you up
destroy
people's lives —
if you
can
choose,
it's not
love

poem

It's terrible
that I don't have
a photo of you
I tried to draw
pictures of you
from memory
but I don't like
any of them
The truth is
that I don't
want a drawing
or a photo
I want you
I need to feel
your hands
on me
and your
tropical
mouth

your face

Late autumn
and your face
is changing
When we met
the air was warm
I saw the wound
beneath your beauty
Sometimes now
when we're together
this scar disappears
and there you are
a young girl again
without pain
Last night, lying
in each other's arms
in your daughter's bed
you asked me,
What will happen
when we're *really*
in love?
I only know
I adore you more
every day
that the wind
won't blow the leaves
back onto the branches

(cont.)

My love, it's
late autumn
and my face
is changing, too.

poem

That the thought
of losing you
is even in my head
disturbs me
I've never cared
for anyone
in this way before
never thought
that I could make
such a mistake
to fall in love
with the real girl
of my dreams
Now it's too late
the hunter captured
by the game
You sleep
with my soul
in your mouth
When we kiss
I can taste it

a dream

As I told you
last night
we were walking
in a dark forest
we got lost
from each other
I had to find you
I called your name
you answered
but your voice
was faint
as if you were suddenly
impossibly far away
I followed the sound
for what seemed
like days
I didn't want
to give up
to leave you alone
in the forest
I didn't know if
you were really lost
or where I was
Finally, I saw you
walking along a path
I didn't know was there
You stopped by a tree

I waited to see
which way you would go
I heard a noise
behind me
and looked around
but nothing moved
Now you were
beside me
and we moved together
along the path
You took my hand
It's true, you said,
I'm a little lost
I followed you anyway
The path disappeared
but we kept going
This is love, I said
You turned and kissed me
Yes, you said, I know.

my last sonnet

I don't know if you remember me,
I'm the boy you danced with
at the Communist picnic in Albarese
We were so in love the bad music
didn't matter, or the weather, clothes glued
to our bodies by sweat as we swirled
Your brothers, their wives and children
seemed amazed by us, the way we danced,
how happy we were—
What happened, my love?
How did we fall?
I feel like Icarus, wings gone
sinking in the sea under the terrible weight
of his father's heart

brigands

Your dream of Sardinia—
you were there once
at fifteen
Your older brother
taught in a village,
married a Sardinian girl
You ran by the sea,
listened to tales of bandits—
briganti—
hiding in the mountains,
only women in the villages—
The *briganti* sneak down
at night
to visit—
your fantasy to be stolen
away, held
captive, ravished, used
by rough men,
one day taught to
fire a gun—
rifle over your shoulder,
barefoot
brigand girl—
You should have gone back
alone, years ago
when Sardinia
and you
were still wild

life & death with an actress

Your idea
of love
is
Duel in the Sun
your ideal
woman
Kleist's Penthesilea
who killed
Achilles
then ate
him
Spared now the burden
of having to die
to prove
my love
I hereby abdicate
this role
in which I was
involuntarily
if not unwittingly
cast
Take pity
if you can
on
my replacement
may he
be agile
as Achilles
but fearful

letter from la habana

Imagine lying in bed
three in the morning
with a pretty mulatta,
she sings for me
a romantic tune
from her not distant childhood
as waves slither
along the beach
accompanying a little wind—
I think of
savage Penthesilea
in Kleist's story, crazed
by unexpected desire
to destroy her chance
at happiness, misunderstanding
Achilles' submission,
devouring him
with her dogs, doomed
thereafter, a ghost of love—
I understand you now,
my Cuban girl's song
lost to myth, the elegant night
caught in her impossible throat.

unsent letter from la habana

In the Cuban night
color of Havana Club
I stared at the black sea
raising itself above the Malecón
an ancient, stubborn beast
trying again and again
to climb ashore
to get back to where
once he had been
And I thought of you
dancing in that beautiful room
high above the white streets
of San Francisco
while I played the piano
looking out a window at clouds
color of sand at Varadero
How to get back, I thought
what miserable beasts we are
how impossibly stubborn
to be in love forever

boca chica

It was all a long time ago
walking next to you
beside you
dropping behind
a little
to watch your ass
as if one fist were
being placed over the other
stepping like a cat
your mother said
Arabs stopped to look
Were we on the Boulevard Magenta?

I wanted it
right there
in front of everyone
or no one
I got it later
only it was so
long ago
I don't remember

shooting pool in the dark

Living with you
is like shooting pool
in the dark
impossible to guess correctly
which ball to hit next
or even know what stripe
or solid, number or color
is still there or where
Life with you is like
being asked to run
a neverending table
blindfolded and bleeding
from a shotgun wound
I once saw Willie Mosconi
run 91 balls in a row
shooting straight pool
at Benzinger's in Chicago
I'd bet anything
he couldn't have done it
with a hole
this size
in his heart

true love

Your sickness made me
a little sick, it's
true—I still
feel it
   Mayakovsky got down
      on his knees
  and declared
            his love
 to his last
          mistress
     a few hours after
        he'd met her
Remember me
at the hotel
          in Paris,
     on my knees
      in the lift?
We're all the same
men of too much passion
and a little talent—
   some a little more
          than others
   We fool ourselves
     into thinking
            we're strong
        then complain
      the rest of our lives
         crippled by
          the consequences

memento

I miss seeing the magnolia
tree
in the courtyard
out the kitchen window
every morning
I remember how upset
you were
after its limbs
were trimmed
I was away when it happened
you were afraid
I'd be unhappy
to see it
but seeing you
was all that mattered
The magnolia
did look sad
nude and frightened
shivering even in
the Roman sun
and you
trembling in my arms
a perfect
fallen
blossom

3

As If It Were a Photograph

Poems after Vermeer

woman in blue reading a letter

She is pregnant
I'm certain
and the letter
is from her husband
a merchant traveling
on the continent
It's possible
that he will not
be with her when
the child is born
and that the child
is not his

the milkmaid

Holding the pitcher
her blue skirt
broad forehead
bread and milk
thick light
pours out

woman with a water jug

Unlike the milkmaid
this woman is
happy
perhaps unconvinced
of the permanence
of her condition
at least she appears
confident and aware
of the importance
if not the meaning
of light

girl asleep at a table

Perhaps she's
not drunk
merely fallen asleep
in an empty house
soon roused
by thunder
to stand for a moment
and watch the rain
on the rooftops
of Delft
before closing
the window
There was once
a dog in the doorway
but Vermeer painted
it out

diana and her companions

Having one's feet washed
is one of life's
greatest pleasures
Diana's powerful arm
protruding breasts
early evening
in Heaven

christ in the house of martha and mary

Red and gold surround
Martha's deranged eye
Mary offering
the loaf
eyes closed
as if it were
a photograph

the procuress

Vermeer and his friends
of the four only Vermeer
looks at the camera
as the picture is taken
he is disengaged
raising a glass
to himself
unaware of his friend's
hand on the whore's
brilliantly yellow breast

officer with a laughing girl

The topographical map of Holland
made by Balthasar van Berckenrode
an open window
dashing soldier
simple girl
nothing between them
but dust in
the light

woman reading a letter at an open window

Figure reflected in
window glass
as she reads
shadow engulfs
her drooping
golden head

the glass of wine

He pours
she drinks
lute on
a chair
wood, porcelain,
silk

the little street

Women and children
broken red clouds
details of
immaculate quiet

woman and two men

Only one pays
her attention
the other despairs
The woman
is not lovely
the man supporting
her hand is
grotesque,
capable of
murder

woman with a pearl necklace

Her self-fascination
is exceeded
in intensity
only by the extent
of our perspective
on her isolation

woman weighing gold

It is because we die
that nothing lasts
There is nothing
profound in
The Last Judgment
gold, strings
of pearls are
no less limited
in value by
their replaceability

the music lesson

Music, companion of
joy, balm
of sorrow
the woman stands
at the keyboard
face reflected
in the mirror
white pitcher on a tray
on a table covered
with a red tapestry
the feeling is
of late afternoon
a delicate hour

the concert

We see the beginnings
of her hands
an accompanist
audience of one
patterned tiles
keep our distance
the painting
unlistenable

girl with a pearl earring

A puzzle
with blue and gold
Arab headwrapping
long earring
face of alabaster
startling
green eyes

the art of painting

Why are Clio's
eyes closed
History inspires
pedants
lips and eyes
measuring devices
of dreams

lady writing a letter

This woman
is well to do
and unafraid
she wears the confident
air of good fortune
Her husband is
not to see this letter
Vermeer's
women disguise
their infidelities
poorly

lady with her maidservant

The maid delivers
a letter from
the lady's lover
the lady's surprise
is undisguised
she could not
be dressed
more elegantly
the maid more drab
or knowing
undisguised, also,
disgust

redux

Walking in Kensington Gardens
with a beautiful girl after rain
I was last here fifteen years ago
walking through this park
with another woman I haven't seen
London doesn't seem much different
nor does the way I go
about living my life
There's something reassuring
about that, even the color
of the sky is as
I remember it, like the light
on the wall over Vermeer's
Lady Reading A Letter

4

Versions of Neveu

Poems by Gérald Neveu

Translated by Barry Gifford

Gérald Neveu

born 10 August 1921
in Marseilles
died 28 February 1960
in Paris

Barry Gifford

born 18 October 1946
in Chicago
died____________

---

for this time

Lifted up between the men
from between the confetti-like streaks of water
Hauled
to the edge of the appointed
Blood, saturated
with terror, calm

To this engulfed face
all the good things they are owed
All the things to be decided
in the violet teachings of regret

But what regret?

The night passes from hand to hand
like love

from the bottom of the tears

Anxieties devoured him
from his tense head at dawn
The rain rocked him
death avenged him

In the hollow of the hand
a trap
a living mirror for the sky
a pure walnut
with the only mystery
of tenderness and sorrow

some part

He is on his knees
for that is not the way
He is on his knees
a star on each wound

His voice confuses him finally
with the sky
a poor little sky
of this world

He is on his knees in the world
near a table of food
When night comes it passes unnoticed

an essential solitude

I thank you my heart
I thank you for making me love
Insofar as in life
You make me love—tell them—
My heart
If this was true
I thank you my heart until in death
Between the weeds
Of sad evenings of this world
Where man risks his life.
I thank you my heart
From the heart of the cluster
Where sweetly slopes the sword of blood
Among the crap and the lawyers
Among the eyes
Which are artlessly striped—avalanche—
My slow movement
Around the estuaries of the handle.

reflection *to Nadine*

When I was small
The lark inclined on the radio
Illuminated me
I laughed wetly like a soup

There was nothing more
To the turn of the street
Than a splash

And we marry
Below
In the sky of the stream

Hands joined
From the past to the future
They're transparent
Like laughing children.

palimpsest

Forgotten day
Opaque speech of trees of birds
Of stones
Of men too
Colors: plural without names
And this architectural ridge
All is learned: old childhood

In moving the walls are black
And these giant whirlwinds that are not
    fountains of noise

Far away strong in itself
A great harp of crisis

A dawn
The only one
And which crosses the body
In a grand display of anguish

O day *almost* forgotten.

customs

Why this child of the hill
bound to the dusk?
Why this filthy child
This sword naked and disgusting?

Grasses without remembrance
Grinding from the water
There where the sea is
Under the faces

Why
this child in hell
and this finger this lone finger
against the dead temples.

epiphany for Gérald Neveu

A truck hauling a palm tree
though the Luxembourg Gardens
Dozens of pretty girls, as always
A few classic bums dozing
against the museum wall
Soon-no-longer-young men reading
magazines, feigning disinterest
sneaking peeks from corners of their eyes
The apartment at the top of the building
on the corner of the Avenue de l'Observatoire
reigns over the park like a mountain peak
I've wanted to live there ever since
I first saw it twenty-five years ago
Today I imagine a faded beauty
wearing only a leopard skin brassiere
and jewel-rimmed dark glasses
looking down at us, surveying her domain
through a powerful telescope
Sudden squeals of schoolgirls
trading photographs under the branches
alert the drowsers on wire chairs
The sky is no longer dead
My most understanding readers
as well as yours
have yet to be born

5

THE LAST WORDS OF ARTHUR RIMBAUD

Place: The Hospital of the Immaculate Conception, Marseilles, France.

Time: November 9, 1891. The day before Rimbaud's death.

ARTHUR RIMBAUD, *37 years old, the poet and adventurer, lies dying in a hospital bed. He drifts in and out of consciousness, delirious with pain. His right leg has been amputated due to a malignancy.*

At his bedside sits his sister, ISABELLE RIMBAUD, *31 years old. The bed is surrounded by candles, flickering in the otherwise darkened room.*

ARTHUR: Tell them, tell them... say that I am entirely paralyzed, yes, and so I wish to embark early. Please let me know at what time I should be carried on board.

ISABELLE: My poor Arthur, it's impossible for you to travel. You can't be moved.

ARTHUR: I'll return to Harar, to Djami, he'll be waiting. I'll return with limbs of steel, dark skin and furious eyes. With this mask, people will think I am of a strong race.

ISABELLE: Forget Djami, forget him. I'm here, Isabelle, your sister. Think of me, of our mother, the ones who love you most.

ARTHUR: My name carved in stone at Luxor, only the wind and sand can erase it. Tell Djami I am coming, I will see him again soon. My one friend, my only friend.

ISABELLE: Djami cannot help you, Arthur. That boy is far from here, in Abyssinia. Probably dead.

ARTHUR: Send him money, three thousand francs. Tell him his master, who loves him, begs he make wise use of this sum, that he invest it prudently in an enterprise sure to realize a profit. Tell him not to be idle. His wife and child must prosper.

ISABELLE: Arthur, pray. Forget Africa.

ARTHUR: Djami and I...two ghosts...slipping through the subtle air. Sons of the sun.

ISABELLE: All the years away from France, broiling in the heat, your brain was affected.

ARTHUR: Capsule rifles, two thousand-forty at fifteen Marie-Therese dollars each. Sixty thousand Remington cartridges at sixty dollars the thousand. Tools of various kinds valued at five thousand-eight hundred dollars. Total value of caravan forty thousand. Fifty days to Menelek, king to pay us on arrival. We leave from Tadjoura. Ivory, musk, gold. The Choans would have our testicles! French testicles. Harar to Antotto, twenty days. Avoid Dankalis, evil savages. Sixty thousand dollars, exchange at Aden, 4.3 francs, equals 258,000 francs. Coffee or slaves. Won't take Egyptian piasters. Caravans form at Djibouti. Did I marry the Somali girl? She went back, Djami sent her away. Not my orders. Find Djami, quick! My leg, must rest my leg before meeting the Emir. Turks and cannons.

ISABELLE: [*praying*] Oh Lord, I weep! Lord, soften his agony. Help him to bear his cross. Have pity on my brother, his poor soul that writhes on earth. Have pity and take him, oh Lord. You who are so good, so kind.

ARTHUR: The hyenas laugh at us. Their laughing keeps me awake. Smelling my wound. Poetry poured from the open wound, words spilled until there was nothing left. Emptied, I fled. Djami, your warmth. She is far off, master, to BarAbir. Far, far. Cannot go there with accounts due. The business. Cheated by Menelek, cunning, cunning. *Le Bosphore Egyptien*, my case. Ragged, dirty rags, no way for a French citizen. Dead before my time, the late Arthur Rimbaud. I have been bitten by life before and survived. Two terrible years and nothing to show.

ISABELLE: Arthur, do you know me? Do you know your sister, your youngest sister, Isabelle? Can you feel my strength, my love? The love of the Lord that flows through me.

ARTHUR: I see you, my angel. My angel of happiness.

ISABELLE: Oh, yes! Yes, Arthur! I am! Your angel. Oh, thank you, Lord, for bringing my brother home before... before....

ARTHUR: Before his death. The death of the late Arthur Rimbaud.

ISABELLE: No, perhaps it is possible that you may live! The Lord is merciful, it's in His power to heal.

ARTHUR: We'll walk then, you and I, around Harar, when my new leg is attached, my artificial limb. You won't believe the colors! And Aden, we'll journey to Aden. I can arrange things there, arms for the South. Tell Djami, my man, my one brother under the sun, I am on my way! I'm coming with snow on my scarf, flowers from the Ardennes, things he's never seen! Wake me before the harbor burns. It will burn after our boat departs, so we can watch the flames from the deck as we disappear over the horizon, a spectacle of fire, our farewell.

ISABELLE: Arthur, Arthur! Are you gone?

ARTHUR: Sails... yellow, red... the sea.

END

about the author

Barry Gifford's novels have been translated into twenty-five languages. His book *Night People* was awarded the Premio Brancati in Italy, and he has been the recipient of awards from PEN, the National Endowment for the Arts, the American Library Association, and the Writers Guild of America. David Lynch's film *Wild at Heart,* which was based on Gifford's novel, won the Palme d'Or at the Cannes Film Festival in 1990; and his novel *Perdita Durango* was made into a feature film by Spanish director Alex de la Iglesia in 1997. Barry Gifford co-wrote with director David Lynch the film *Lost Highway* (1997); he also co-wrote with director Matt Dillon the film *City of Ghosts* (2003). Mr. Gifford's recent books include *The Phantom Father,* named a *New York Times* Notable Book of the Year; *Wyoming,* named a *Los Angeles Times* Novel of the Year, which has been adapted for the stage and film; *Do the Blind Dream?*; *American Falls: The Collected Short Stories*; and *The Rooster Trapped in the Reptile Room: A BARRY GIFFORD READER.* Mr. Gifford's writings have appeared in *Punch, Esquire, Rolling Stone, Sport,* the *New York Times, El Pais, Reforma, La Repubblica, Projections* and many other publications. He lives in the San Francisco Bay Area. For more information please visit www.barrygifford.com.